# Let's Talk,

# Let's Play

by

Jane Winslow Eliot

Published by:
**The Association of Waldorf Schools of North America**
**3911 Bannister Road**
**Fair Oaks, CA 95628**

# Let's Talk, Let's Play

Author: Jane Winslow Eliot

Editor: David Mitchell

Proofreader: Nancy Jane

ISBN # 0-9623978-9-X

Curriculum Series

The Publications Committee of AWSNA is pleased to bring forward this publication as part of its Curriculum Series. The thoughts and ideas represented herein are solely those of the author and do not necessarily represent any implied criteria set by AWSNA. It is our intention to stimulate as much writing and thinking as possible about our curriculum, including diverse views. Please contact us with feedback on this publication as well as requests for future work.

David S. Mitchell
For the Publications Committee
AWSNA

# Contents

## Part One

## Let's Talk

# Part Two

## Let's Play

## Games

## Music for Games

# Part One

# Let's Talk

### RHYTHM

  In one year the earth circles the sun. The moon orbits the earth in twenty-eight days. The earth rotates in a twenty-four hour spin. These orbits, and uncountable others, are held in a wheel which takes thousands of years to whirl around just once. And yet all these motions roll in rhythm and affect us.

  An adult who wishes to guide a child into this world with the least damage possible can do no better than to choose to work with rhythm. When you place your children in rhythm with the universe, they are well prepared to behave harmoniously. Later, they will seek original and individual ways to contribute to the ongoing adventure of the human race — creating their own new circles while still remaining in synch.

  Rhythm is one of the most useful tools a parent or teacher will ever come across because rhythm helps to contain a person, just like a glass shapes water, no matter how scattery, or how willful water can potentially be.

3

By rhythm I don't mean music only, although music is included in all world rhythms. Songs have lately taken over from books as the form in which many ideas meet the growing child. However, when you seek out as many rhythms as you can, you store magical tools with which to work with your children. Think of the rhythms of the day, that is, day and night — a twenty-four hour segment. It is the time it takes for the earth to revolve just once, and the sun to rise, then set, just once. Familiarity with these facts, not just intellectually, and not merely through picture books, but through experience in their daily lives, helps children harmonize with the dominant rhythms of our globe. When are in tune with such motions, they feel the deep reassurance that cosmic harmonies bring about.

Imagine it first yourself.

For instance, note the differences in the kind of energy at a child's disposal. See how children tend to bounce into the world each morning with enough energy to zonk an elephant — often on your chest. It's called the dawn effect. If all goes well, it will have been used up during the day and will need to be replenished that night in sleep. Between waking and sleeping, that is between high energy times and low ones, the parent may notice something very simple: active children need outlets for all that energy. Well, just because that fact tends to be ignored doesn't mean it isn't obvious. What is less obvious is that the energy changes many times throughout a day. For instance, children tend to learn more in the morning. Their brains are ready to accept new information, they can help around the house with greater vigor, and they play outside with courage. Their will is fresh. Awakening to a new day, they come prepared to meet life as if it had purpose. As the sun crosses the heights of heaven, a change takes place. A dreamier side takes over. "Let's pretend" games, maybe a nap or a picture book on a bed, or quiet painting times, are welcomed. Later still, seemingly pointless, formless activities with friends, or outdoor play, baking with a grownup, humorous activities, little playlets, all make for afternoon fun.

As the sun's energies are shielded behind the earth, and bedtime approaches, evening lulls their loosening wills. Children are pulled towards separation from their earth-bound bodies. Then pleasant times with elders and quiet gentling into sleep are in order. Song, poetry, prayer, comforting stories, and simple rituals reassure the nodding child. The little beings who have held themselves intact all day long are easily scattered now. It is hard for them to hold themselves together. Their need to replenish energies is apparent. If you let things slip and become turbulent at this time, children may find it difficult to edge through the window of sleep that opens so narrowly and so softly.

Ritual is a form of rhythm. Ritual repeats events and allows for confidence in the expected. Ritual, like rhythm, tends to create a mood in which the children rest in wonder. As you create the gentle moods that rituals can evoke, you activate reverence instead of rough-housing. In rituals the hands and face-washing, toothbrushing, putting on PJs, tidying toys, dinner at the same time each night (as often as possible), all can become parts of ritual when met in a spirit of gentle respect for children and their needs. This mundane repetition of daily practices is as much a part of the eternal return as candlelight, songs, chants, poems, or prayer. All soothe the rhythms of the blood and slow the breath from highspeed excitement to unhurried joy. Images of the goodness of the day past, of stars in their right places in the sky, a silver moon on high, angels in heaven or nearby, blessings poured down while one sleeps, all relax the sleepyheads. They feel secure. As breath slows, and hearts beat regularly, peacefulness steals over them. They are enchanted by the gentle expectedness of their life with you. They are home safe.

It's worth a try.

Of course, you will have to decide how you wish to shape your days. And there is little chance that any routine you set up will remain unbroken. However, working with the rhythms of the day gets easier as you go along and see for yourself how they help in the simple problems all parents face: the relentless fact of three meals a day; the bath, the hair, the dishes, the sweeping, the tidying; getting to school on time, or dressed, and all the rest — details which add up to very busy times for all concerned.

Once you feel the daily pulse, there are the seasons to consider: fall, winter, spring, and summer. One needs to sense the deep stirrings within the earth and relate to them in daily activities. Birthdays mark the sun's rhythm, and an individual one, too. There are longer periods, such as seven year chunks to take into consideration, but that is another story.

Rhythm, rhythm, rhythm. If the children learn to expect something, so it doesn't seem to come as an arbitrary order from you, but is almost as predictable as night and day, they are likely to slide right into the activity on a song rather than on a whimper.

It's a miracle not to be missed.

Rhythm is an anti-gravity device, protecting children from the crushing pull of the material world. It re-invigorates the will and clears the imagination. Rhythm brings the expected with freshness, too. It makes the familiar new each time. Since children have to face new challenges every day of their little lives, familiarity is a welcome base from which to meet the unknown. Familiarity makes obstacles and frustrations less intimidating. Things do work out. In a home where rhythm carries routine, children learn this out of their own experience.

One of the most practical aids in working with rhythm is poetry, as you will see in the next chapter. Poetry is a natural part of human communication and takes us to the furthest reaches of human spirit. Through poetry we touch the hidden recesses of the unformed heart. Poetry will help our children (and ourselves) to endeavor beyond the expected. The feeling which remains when even the simplest poem is ended is one of hope: "I, too, can explore and shape the mysteries of the human spirit; I, too will add to its power and glory; I, too, will matter to my world."

Because children long to become adults, watch what you give them to imitate. You are the guardian of the oral tradition, the keeper of the secrets of our past. You are the elder, bringing the world to the newcomer. However foolish, inefficient you may feel, the child longs to grow up "to be like you." If that makes you feel inadequate, don't worry, things will interfere. Children will become more like themselves than like you, if all goes well. In the meantime, share what you know as wonderfully and as gently as you can — in rhythm.

## Uses of Poetry

Poetry is well-shaped emotion. It is well-practiced motion. And it is practical, too. Poetry helps a child to read, to write, to speak clearly, to remember, to develop subtle self-control in body motion, to balance feelings, and much more.

> A bird flew down on silent wing,
> We hushed ourselves to hear him sing.
> Because we hushed, he flew away.
> He only sings when we will play.

In this poem Ethel Cook Eliot helps children feel that what they are doing when "just playing" is natural and good. The adult world subtly validates the fact that they are doing the right thing at the right time.

Before children appreciate beauty or understand truth, they feel immense delight in the good. Here is a poem which can be used right from the day a child is born:

Goodnight, Goodnight,
Far flies the light,
But still God's love
Does shine above
Making all bright,
Goodnight, Goodnight.

Seek poems about:
Nature
Seasons
Festivals
Numbers
Letters
Being small
Being funny
Being right, doing right, feeling right

Although we often fail to do so, it is not so hard for an adult to respect the quality of littleness — if we think about it.

Today we can easily find traditional songs and games on records for children. It is a good idea to use these to refresh one's memory if need be, but it is well to caution against giving them to children. There are many reasons for this, but in the context of games we can narrow in on the human voice. When one person speaks to another, the sound has a healing, reassuring quality that will help a child grow strong. Not only the words or the meaning of the words fills a child with a deep bliss, but there is the feeling of being surrounded, protected in some non-physical way. A child playing in a field while a parent sings will seldom stray beyond the range of the song, held happily in the security of the human voice.

How can we share with each other the complexities of the adult world if we do not start somewhere to celebrate the power of the spoken word — the word given from one human to another? The word hurts when it is harsh, heals when it is soothing, and is more nutritive than any food except mother's milk. Even when sung off tune, or said ungrammatically, the spoken word will do more for a child than any number of smoothly recorded, impersonal, detached, entertaining, machine-dominated discs.

Waldorf school education insists on their teachers creating as much of their material as possible. This brings a special energy into the classrooms. It is like a fresh peach in summer. The children sense when a poem has been formed just for them. It inspires them to emulate the adult. Teachers are then better able to appreciate the powerful initiative brought out in the creative endeavor. With gentle guidance they may help the child find a poetic word. Just as important, teachers help their charges maintain their persistence, so the poem gets finished, and all can partake of the excitement of creation. That first day when light was separated from darkness must have been something like children's happiness when their first poems are presented to their class.

Here is a Waldorf teacher's poem which teaches about springtime. In it Jane Johansen sweetly describes spring excitement, along with its beauty and mystery. By the way, spring itself is a performance of persistence and creativity.

*CATERPILLAR*
Caterpillar creeps so smoothly
Over twigs and under flower,
In the air and curling lightly
Round into his leafy bower.
Now he spins his bright cocoon.
Light is weaving all around.
In the dark he's softly dreaming
Fast asleep without a sound.

Children are strongly affected by your love for a poem.
They assume that whatever you bring them of the world is something of importance and therefore magical in some wonderful way. This will lead them to the same affection for the works of others.

Robert Louis Stevenson is another poet whose rhythms are gentle and whose images expansive. The following poem helps a child feel comfortable with the dark. It is appropriate for children five, six and over to learn, but younger children love to hear the soothing, sing-song cadences.

The lights from the parlor and kitchen shone out
    Through the blinds and the windows and bars;
And high overhead and all moving about,
    There were thousands of millions of stars.
There ne'er were such thousands of leaves on a tree,
    Or of people in church or the park,
As the crowds of the stars that looked down upon me,
    And that glittered and winked in the dark.
The Dog, and the Plough, and the Hunter and all,
    And the star of the sailor, and Mars,

These shone in the sky, and the pail by the wall
   Would be half-full of water and stars.
They saw me at last, and they chased me with cries,
   And they soon had me packed into bed;
But the glory kept shining and bright in my eyes,
   And the stars going 'round in my head.

## WONDER

Find verses which fit the open, delicate sense of wonder
that children have at each new stage of development. Children
are transparent and simple, without being simple-minded. Words
and meanings will fuse into the very fibres of a growing child,
but they should also be elastic enough to grow with them, too.
Some poetry expands as the child develops. It then resounds as
deeply at fifty or seventy as at five or seven.

The following poem is by a great poet: William Blake. It is
innocent enough for children over three to sleep on, while being
expansive enough to grow with them for the rest of their lives.

The sun descending in the west,
The evening star does shine.
The birds are silent in their nest,
And I must seek for mine.
   The moon like a flower
   In heaven's high bower,
   With silent delight
   Sits and smiles on the night.

Farewell green fields and happy groves
Where flocks have took delight,
Where lambs have nibbled, silent moves
The feet of angels bright;

11

Unseen they pour blessing
And joy without ceasing
On each bud and blossom
And each sleeping bosom.

## REPETITION

Through repetition you reach the child's feeling life, bringing harmony to restless emotions. A lovely poem carefully selected for nighttime quiets the little one. Agitation left from the day, dread of the oncoming night, can be soothed away by the right poem. The entire responsibility for ending the day no longer falls heavily on the parent. You won't have to say: "Time for me to turn off the light." Instead, the day ends itself in a familiar, solace-filled way which the parent and the child can both accept.

## LISTENING AND HEARING

Listening to poetry makes children feel ennobled. They drift in and out with the words, for those they understand, they really understand with their whole souls, while the others they simply leave for later. If you want your child to grow up with a strong command of language, a most welcomed freedom to have, then it does no harm to start early and bathe them in ennobling words. But do it without forcing the matter; never demand total grasp of the vocabulary. On the contrary, stay ahead of the game so that the child's psyche is embraced in the ever-expanding mystery of speech.

In life, the artistically formed and spoken word is the art of the ego.

Poetry helps children form good listening habits. A person needs training and encouragement to be able to listen easily, with intelligent interest and compassion. Listening is as important as reading, and ought to come first. The habit of listening well leads to good writing skills later on.

A word of caution here: To listen is not the same as to hear. To listen requires your own active participation; hearing is a passive state. You "listen" to the tone in which something is said, whereas you "hear" a loud noise. You listen for the meaning and resonance of the spoken word in its beauty, pacing, gentleness — or their opposites. Whether you are aware of it or not, a part of you listens for the thought behind the tone, the meaning behind the words, whereas your ears hear only sounds. Too often we monitor what is coming in with "I like it" or "I don't like it." But that is not listening. Listening is sympathetic. It means one's self is paying attention to another's self.

## SELECTIONS

Ask yourself questions about each poem. For instance, does it: Merge with the season you are in? Springtime changeability? Summer dreams? Fall initiatives? Winter dedication? Attach to the place you visit or live: city, country, seaside, desert? Honor birthdays, festivals, arrivals, and departures? Describe the character of an animal or plant? Help you empathize with fellow creatures? Engage the will, so a child will go dig, sail, climb, wash, or dance? Create a sense of joyful goodness, wonder and mystery? Meet the deep needs of grief? Is there humor in it so the children laugh easily and for joy?

Not every poem has to do all of these things, but each poem should do one of them. The child will feel: "Here I stand on firm foundation."

Ralph Waldo Emerson contrasts being little with being big and finds both good. Find the rhythm of this unusual poem as it may not jump out at you. Learn it by heart, repeat, and experiment.

The Mountain and the Squirrel had a quarrel;
And the former called the latter 'little Prig.'
Bun replied,
'You are doubtless very big;
But all sorts of things and weather
Must be taken in together
To make up a year
And a sphere.
And I think it no disgrace
To occupy my place.
If I'm not so large as you,
You are not so small as I,
And not half so spry.
I'll not deny you make
A very pretty squirrel track;
Talents differ; all is well and wisely put;
If I cannot carry forests on my back,
Neither can you crack a nut.'

## ORIGINALITY

These poems will take you some time to learn and will take the children months, even years, and that is good. It will mean repetition day after day. In our time, it cannot be emphasized enough that daily repetition is a form of rhythm, and, therefore, brings a healing quality into the lives of the young. Repetition is the secure foundation for healthy originality. Our society is surprised that so many teen-agers seek new experiences at any cost. There is really no cause for surprise. Children too often are conditioned to savor "originality" at an early age. There is little time for a child to rest in the expected and familiar of their own experiences. On the other hand, children learn to trust adults and the universe through repetition and familiarity. They love the familiar. We all do. It is comforting, like a favorite toy. It provides strength, like a well-loved home. Don't be afraid to repeat, even when the child seems to want something new. It is a matter of balance. The truth is that the innermost being of the child longs for the support and safety of the familiar, even while preparing eagerly to tackle the original and challenging.

Poetry, with its clear yet subtle insights and its warmly affirming quality, helps children form the power to make judgments of their own, rather than have judgments thrust upon them. In other words, it leaves children free to form judgments that enhance rather than sterilize life.

The following is a short poem with a loving thought which, through repetition, gentles a child into dream:

> I see the moon,
> The moon sees me.
> God bless the moon,
> God bless me.

## WHEN TO BEGIN

You can begin these poems as early as you choose. The children will love the rhythms, will enjoy your affection for them, and will grow into each one quite naturally, at their own pace. The shining spirit is carried by the words as in golden cups. There is no need for explanations.

## MOTHER GOOSE

People often ask about the value of nursery rhymes, because they find the oddest things in them. Some parents find too much violence, inanity, and irrelevant political satire from ages long past. Of course, it matters what is brought to the vulnerable feeling life of a child under seven. Moreover, it's true that

15

much which stayed alive by hiding in nursery rhymes is meaningless today. Still, when ancient festivals were outlawed and then slowly forgotten, they lingered on as children's games and songs.

Who has not wondered if it were possible to jump over the moon? I bet there was at least one astronaut on that first visit in 1967 who repeated this verse while hurtling towards that magnetic rock. The fact remains that Mother Goose offers wonderful rhythms and images, together with a host of half-glimpsed secrets from ancient days. Most important of all, children love the rhythms of Mother Goose.

> Hey, Diddle Diddle,
> The cat and the fiddle,
> The cow jumped over the moon;
> The little dog laughed
> To see such fun
> And the dish ran away with the spoon.

When the starry Bull, Taurus, appears in a certain area of the night sky, it heralds life-giving springtime once again. Then when "the cow jumps over the moon", its milk-full stomach hides some of the moon's light, leaving only gleaming crescent horns. The coupling stars used to guide farmers in their planting. Even today there are farmers who plant by the light of the stars and the moon. Beets, for instance, are held to be healthiest when planted at the time of a waning moon, with Taurus rising.

When the Cow is jumping, the Big Dipper dipping, or the Hunter lifting his bow in specific relations to the moon, it indicates the beginning, middle or end of a working schedule. Farmers, sailors, hunters all need to know when to plant or sail or hunt for winter stores. When the Cow jumps over the Moon, or the Dog Star laughs, it is time for action. In Egypt, where the Cow goddess was known as Isis, the rising Dog Star signaled the beginning of the yearly life-giving flood of the Nile River. It was time to get things ready for the miraculous planting ahead. In Greece, the Cow Goddess was known as Io. In India a white cow is still sacred, and in parts of Africa, farmers still plant by the stars and the moon. Modern bio-dynamic farmers, work with "the Cow and the Bull and the Hunter and all" in complex procedures. The patient cosmos-reflecting cow is an integral part of a modern bio-dynamic farm. These special techniques have become part of a worldwide approach to modern agriculure.

## FESTIVALS

> Jack and Jill
> Went up the hill
> To fetch a pail of water;
> Jack fell down
> And broke his crown
> And Jill came tumbling after.
> Up Jack got
> And home did trot
> As fast as he could caper;
> He went to bed,
> To mend his head,
> With vinegar and brown paper.

This poem harks back to rituals common all over the world in olden times. On the day of the full moon in the middle month of spring, it was customary to get up at dawn and go collect the early morning dew for use in May Day festivals. Dew gathered on this Moon day was deemed to be particularly potent. It was sacred and had healing properties.

17

The pearl-like drops would insure an abundance of milk from the cows; it would bring prosperity to households; it would protect a woman's beauty and secure a rich harvest. In particular, on the first of May, or May Day, a round cake was made from grains, sheep's milk, and sacred dew. Before coming to the table, this cake was rolled down a sacred hill; and the important thing was for it to reach the bottom intact.

What seems at first glance to have been quaint and aimless ceremony was a communal effort to develop precision in measurement, dexterity in crafting, and skill in manipulating the rolling, round hard-cake. Can you see the elders watching the nine-year-olds to see how they built, baked, and managed their ring-shaped cakes? How the youngsters did might decide their futures. Would they be accepted as apprentices by the blacksmith, the sea captain, the farmer, or the initiate of the temple secrets?

The full moon, the dark of the moon, the first quarter of this spring time, are days which have been held sacred for thousands of years. Fragments of these celebrations have been discovered around the globe, for depending on the location, the phases of the moon announced the abundance of the spring harvest and welcomed summer fruits.

With gentle fun, the festivals once awakened the community to the serious demands of the change of season. Attention was then the watchword, survival the issue. Festivals first served to alert our ancestors to important seasonal changes; then egged them on to do the needed work; and finally inspired them to celebrate their energetic and communal efforts.

Even today, the changing seasons affect not only outward nature but also our inward selves. One does well to meditate on the changes wrought by nature's rounds. Sometimes we are awakened to physical activitiy in the splendid outer world. Sometimes we are led indoors, to study and create, quietly protected from the elements. Always we are part of nature's big and small needs. We can't get out of nature, but we can try to bring our children into full partnership with this fruitful, generous, and most mysterious entity.

## Spring Moon

Have you ever wondered why we have a hare dropping eggs in all western children's baskets when rabbits do not lay eggs? In North America when we look at the brightest moon of the year, spring's full moon, we can find, instead of the Man in the Moon, a Rabbit. In Japan you can clearly discern this rabbit / hare most monthly full moons. But in the West it appears clearly only on the full moon of the spring equinox. See if you can find it. Don't point it out, but let the children look for it themselves. The skies, as so often happens, hold the answer. Before anyone used calendars, pictures and poems were people's memory devices. These were devices to keep alive the life-saving secrets of the returning seasons, which were written so clearly, yet ever mysteriously, in the heavens.

You'll find it's worth your while to build up a whole store of poems from many sources – poems that celebrate a festival, a season, a pet, or a beloved place, for example. These need not all be 'great' poetry, but you want them to have good strong rhymes and rhythms. Sprinkle your selections with gentle humor. If some poems also contain that elusive quality of greatness, better yet. Meanwhile, the simple and anonymous Mother Goose verses remain a treasure-trove.

## Quick Now

When a child suddenly asks for a poem, a story, or a song, you may be caught off-guard. You feel uneasy, unprepared, inadequate. Then the following verse may help to bridge the mo-

19

ment. Either it will give you time to think of something, or else it may itself satisfy just by its good nature and happy rhymes:

> Sing , sing, what shall I sing?
> The cat's run away with the pudding string!
> Do, do, what shall I do?
> The cat has bitten it quite in two !

One needs to go easy on just plain silliness, or course, but on the other hand one does not wish to be too solemn. Many a simple two or four-line rhyme will serve to engage children under five, and leave them feeling satisfied that they have had your full attention for the brief moment required.

## WEATHER

> A sunshiny shower
> Won't last half an hour.

This is true in April and early May. It is also true of a child's tears. They come and go like springtime showers. A kiss, a hug, and a little verse such as that one can put a weepy, bunched up little boy or girl back in shape again, ready to run off into the sunshine and get on with the serious work of play.

> The smell of rain is lovely
> The feel of rain is good
> And once I spent all morning
> With rain in a wood.

Such whimsically reverent verses might inspire you to go out in the rain with the children, rather than calling after them: "Don't get wet!"

three
umbrellas

stood
in
a

corner

(praying
for
rain)

The way Robert Lax sets his poem on the page guides you to its rhythm. Keep trying the slight pauses to plumb all the gentle, wondrous possibilities offered by this transparent picture.

## Alphabet

There are rhymes which help children to remember letters. I used this with my son, Jefferson, substituting Jeff for Jack.

Jack be nimble,
Jack be quick,
Jack jump over the candlestick.

Jump it lively,
Jump it quick,
But don't knock over the candlestick .

All such poems can be recited in pantomine with good, strong gestures.

Too often education makes a child "brainy." Quite literally children become tensely bunched in their brains as a result of being taught too much factual information too soon. Insistent instruction tends to inhibit growth forces from radiating out into lungs and limbs. Powers that were going to spread through the entire child are snapped back into the cranium instead of irradiating the whole body.

## COUNTING

> One, two,
> Button my shoe.
> Three, four,
> Open the door.
> Five, six,
> Pick up sticks.
> Seven, eight,
> Lay them straight.
> Nine, ten,
> Big fat hen.

Number poems can be said while counting on the fingers and toes, or you can stamp and clap them to great effect. Get the counting into the limbs. It strengthens the memory.

## TEMPERAMENTS

Rhythms and meters will help you reach the temperament of a child, tactfully. For instance, while admitting the wide variety of children's moods and attitudes, backgrounds, all children tend to be quick and short-attentioned. A meter which goes / / —, that is short, short, long, reaches children where they are and leads them gently and with fun into other states. The profound effect a change in meter has on a child's pulse and breath is a major reason for using poems as a tool at home or in school. Thinking consciously about meter opens you to the rich veins of ennobling emotion running deep under the surface of even the simplest poetry.

## RHYTHM OF THE DAY

Your choice of poems is most effective when the verses reflect the rhythms of the day. Choose rousing poems in the morning, soothing ones at evening time. You want the child's will to be active in the morning and midday, quieter rhythms in the afternoon, and more reflective elements to the fore as the day winds down.

Here's one for morning:

> Oh, the brave old Duke of York
> He had ten thousand men;
> He marched them up to the top of the hill,
> Then marched them down again.

> Oh, when you are up you are up,
> And when you are down you are down,
> And when you are only halfway up
> You are neither up nor down.

Such a poem is at once rousing, cheerful and yet strongly formed. Pale faces begin to glow warm as the verses encourage every one to stomp heartily up and down the room. Stomping, clapping, and pounding are activities which may be helpful when reciting poetry — if you don't use overkill and wreck the beauty of the poem itself. Rhythmic movement in the body makes for clear speaking in the long run.

Chanting loudly while stamping out poetic metres helps to iron out the wrinkles of frustration which children so often experience. Shyness and inhibition brought about by fear of failure are a terrible burden for a youngster. Stamping in unison with others lets go of some of the knots binding the soul forces.

Strong, energy-rousing rhythms help children stay within their own control, instead of getting lost in boisterous play. Let them be boisterous on occasion, of course, but give them this kind of chanting as an alternative kind of energetic activity so they can see how much skill they need to achieve direction over their own powers. Thus, they come to sense the rhythmic possibilities of their bodies. They feel themselves right into their fingers and toes.

## TRAVEL

Poems offer opportunities to travel with children in imagination through space and time. Verse will transport a child back to some special moment in history or out to some distant sea. These are great to chant when travelling.

When my children were six and seven, Alex and I took them around the world — mostly by freighter. As we were sailing along the southwest coast of India, the legendary coast of Malabar, we chanted this Stevenson verse:

> Where shall we adventure today that we're afloat,
> Wary of the weather, and steering by a star?
> Shall it be to Africa, a-steering of the boat,
> To Providence, or Babylon, or off to Malabar?

It doesn't have to be so exotic, though. Poems can be chanted in the car or on the plane on the way to visiting grandparents or friends. Find poems about your town, state, river, or valley. You can also use poetry to prepare for a move to a new home, anticipating summer visits to seaside or country, going to

24

school, and the like. If you can't put your hands on one, make it up for the occasion. It's not as difficult as it seems at first. It does not have to be a masterpiece, and it comes easier after you have done a few. Just remember your children will prefer one of your own to a 'good' one by the best.

It's encouraging.

## FAMILY AND FESTIVALS

One may be lucky and have a published poet in the family, but in any case, it is worthwhile to find out what poems family members have indeed written. These often display sincerity and warm feeling for the immediate, which children cherish.

Here is an example of a festival poem which we still say in my family. It's a Christmas poem by my grandmother, Ada Davenport Kendall:

My Christmas Tree, you may surmise,
Is hung about with Christmas pies;
With candy canes and barley sticks;
With thank-you-ma'ams and kümmelwicks.

On it you'll find the prayers you've said,
The dreams you've dreamed, your daily bread;
Your Sunday cake, your hopes come true,
And all the things you'd like to do.

The joys you've shared; the gifts you've sent
To others, and all the hours you've spent
Just loving him and her and me ;
All shine in beauty on the tree.
Sweet Christmas time,
Bright Christmas cheer,
A happy day
A blessed year.

In affirming that things are right, that the world and people are one, and that the world is good, poetry cannot help but reinforce children's wellbeing. While learning a variety of verses, children are told that life will need their participation and unique qualities. Without self-conscious explanations, children will absorb both your reverence for the mysteries of life and your mood of quiet delight in poetry's power.

## ONE LAST POEM FOR YOU

Children need poetry. For that matter, so do we. Marketing, washing, cleaning, cooking, entertaining, caring, a career, and the never-ending activities of a day or a week get a parent down sometimes. We feel a little like the giant Atlas did when he carried the world on his shoulders. There came a time when Atlas wished someone would share his burden. When Herakles appeared and carried the load for awhile, Atlas was overjoyed. Parents need to get some of the accumulated weight of the world off their shoulders, if only by letting some of the chores go, simplifying their lives, and being less demanding of themselves.

When I came to this point, as all parents do, I found great joy, freedom, and support in this Robert Lax poem. One doesn't always have to think big. It doesn't all rest on your shoulders. Ask yourself, did you really make your child? Or is there more? Is it not still a mystery? Still, if there is more, there's obviously more you can count on. So let go sometimes. Feel your smallness in the face of all greatness. Relax and let go.

Then Robert Lax's poem can drift through your heart, helping you let go:

a
small
wave

says
a

small

thing

to
the

shore

Sometimes you may feel small but sometimes that may be
big enough.

# Part Two

# Let's Play

It was the longest day of the year – time to celebrate Midsummer's Day, the festival which announces the first day of summer. It is the time when the earth's forces of expansion are at their strongest. In Europe it is often celebrated with fairs, processions, dances, plays, and games. In many countries great bonfires are built near the villages, sometimes on scores of surrounding hills, often taking six weeks in the making. As the fires begin to burn, sparks fly up into the shimmering midsummer's night like spirits trying to get to heaven. When the fires burn low, the brave, the agile, and the foolhardy try to jump the embers for good luck. The pines up the mountainsides are bright with new growth, sprouting like candles on a christmas tree.

This particular sunny afternoon we were celebrating the day with a festival at a Waldorf school I was helping to start in New England. The grownups were languid, while the children were indefatigable, like sparks on a bonfire, or butterflies among the buttercups. They scattered and scampered, ran, romped, and rough-housed. They danced outrageously in procession and sang loudly. So it was with some curiosity that I watched one little five-year-old stand very still and alone almost at the center of the swirls of colorfully costumed people. He gazed up at a magnificent sunflower which towered several feet above him, waiting intently. The great sunflower leaned over as if showering beams of sunlight down from its spiraling pattern of sunflower seeds. The sun silhouetted the two figures as they stood quietly but firmly in the scattery, chattery bustle of the summer afternoon.

Curious, I went to talk to his teacher, Katerina. "Oh," she explained, laughing happily. "He is having a sunflower shower." It seemed that one of the class activities this past week had been to have the children line up in front of the sunflower and each take a turn at a sunflower shower. I was witnessing the effect it had had on this dreamy child. Quiet, self-contained, respectful, the child drew strength from the fruitful plant world – no shaking of the stem, no pulling of the leaves, no attempt to pick at the seeds. This was direct, full-hearted communication, expansive, to go with the warm-heartedness of the season.

The Greek philosopher Heraclitus once said that "all things are in flux." Children certainly are. Sprightly, fluttery, industrious, adventurous, children and their relentless push-pull of energy will leave a grownup gasping. It is as if they live in motion: motion demanded by the physical world, but also motion pressing from their inner selves. As their guides and allies, we cherish both kinds. We merely work to bring these energies within the children's own power — gently, and with good humor.

## MOTION AND INNER MOTION

When you think of inner motion, don't think only emotion and make the mistake of locating only your feelings. There is plain inner motion, too, pulsing eternally, which you will find

29

helpful to know about. Your children in turn will be gratefull for your guidance in bringing inner motion effectively within their power to direct.

The first thing is to locate this motion within yourself. Then, in the next chapter, you will find some games to start you off with the children.

Try closing your eyes and standing on one leg. You will see immediately how unguided inner movement tends to unbalance you. Outer motion is easier to grasp. For instance, with eyes open, try to walk a straight line. You'll quickly see that it takes attention to your body and its relation to the world to do it well for any length of time. But it's not truly difficult.

Next visualize a foot race: children see the goal, check the competition, hear the starter, then run with all the strength of their little bodies. The winning or losing will depend, however, as much on the competition as on one's own abilities. This is outer activity. It calls for willpower and judgment. You test, then compete against yourself or another. You act in the world.

Now watch a child playing "Let's Pretend." Using a chair and an old blanket, the child invites a host of invisible friends, talks to them, entertains them, maybe discovers foreign lands with them, sometimes fights with them, then sends them all away well-fed and happy. Theirs is inner movement, found with the eyes of imagination, plus ears, hands, and all the rest, too. This kind of motion is non-competitive, filled with images and feelings. There are no set goals, no real beginning or end. However, with compassionate attention you are witnessing the dynamics of another's inner life.

While physical acts usually trail visual thinking, it is story which infuses the gestures of the "Let's Pretend" game. The imaginative side is much less emphasized in games having to do with competition, or physical prowess, although that is chang-

30

ing as coaches in a great many professional sports adopt guided visualization as a tool to enhance performance.

It's all a matter of balance.

## BALANCE

All forms of motion make for a well-balanced person. When we use imagination and what we know about rhythm, working them together harmlessly, children will learn to harmonize motion, emotion, and inner motion together in wonderful new ways. This power will be a healing skill to have when they are ready to enter our world as independent beings.

As allies and guides to our children, we will want to know how we can address these motions so that we enhance them, and also how to harmonize them so that they work together.

Aren't these activities what we often call balance? Isn't this what athletes achieve, much to our admiration? And don't we usually admire a well-balanced person?

Balance is a human skill we all like to have. But how, when we are so often a-flutter and a-swirl, can we help our children locate personal balance?

A harmless, fun-filled way is through the power of the spoken word when working with games, songs, poetry, rhythm, and imagination.

Inner and outer movement have been kept separate in the past, except by artists, saints, and people with a cause, but they are really different paths to the same center. We are not two, or three; each one of us is one. What happens too often is that we get stuck on just one chosen path, either following the holy grails of inspiration, the castles in air of imagination, or the brass rings of physical life, as if these paths belonged to three different people. And yet our speech reveals that they intertwine:

31

We aspire to great heights.
We fly away with excitement.
We are beside ourselves with anger.
We are on tip-toes with anticipation.
We can think our way out of a paper bag.
We drown in tears.
Joy expands us.

These are emotions and inner motions revealed by outer motion. As children develop good humor, courage, and compassion, they will be able to bring all these turbulent churnings within their own capacities. No more will we have to hear: "He's an intellectual." Or: "I'm a feeling sort of person." Or: "She's all will." Our children will be all three. They will have warm, compassionate thoughts, clear, thoughtful feelings towards others, proved out in fullhearted action.

## VISUAL THINKING AND IMAGINATION

One way to work and play with inner and outer motion is by using the faculty now called visual thinking. We used to call it imagination, and it often seems wild and unreal. I think that's why the new language tries to cool it down by naming it "visual thinking." However, it is just as much a seeing faculty as it is a thinking one. In fact, imagination has the power to help you see what is really in the world around you, and so be able to deal with it in healing, healthy ways. Imaginative insight into the world leads directly to action. It strengthens your will to action. So imaginative insight needs the ground of compassion. Lacking compassion we create a desert of personal selfishness around ourselves. A self without the three powers of vigorous visual thinking, compassionate imaginative insight into the world, and the healing power of empathetic action becomes like those little grey ghost icons on a computer screen when the program is turned off: inefficient and ineffectual.

## PRACTICE FOR YOU

Here are some easy exercises for you to loosen your imagination, so that you become inventive in playing with your children:

Since imagination activates inner motion, sense this inner activity and use it for surprising initiatives. For instance: stand with feet together, hands by the sides. Slowly curl yourself into a scrunched up ball, arms and hands clenching around your abdomen as you squat down. Then slowly uncurl until you are standing high up on tiptoes, with arms outstretched, fingers wiggling. Now do this while imagining you are an acorn then an oak tree, or anything that contracts and expands.

Imagine being steam, then imagine being ice. What gestures would you use? How does it feel?

Imagine being a great oak tree, strong and full. Then be a tiny acorn. Feel the contraction, act it out. Then return to being a standing tree again, rooted in the ground, branches free in the breeze.

Imagine being a dandelion, then a seed flying away, then contracting into the earth of a cold autumn field. Come back to standing as a human being.

Sense the difference between the contraction and expansion when you do the motions with and without imaginations.

These exercises will confirm the way in which imagination is tied to inner motion, and how flexible it makes you. When you play with your children in a thoughtful, tactful, perceptive, fun manner, you, too, will find life more free and fun, because children make a game of everything.

It's the way to grow.

# RING GAMES

What is the mood the children live in when playing Ring Games? A ring is all eternal rounds: the starry zodiac, the flat, comforting horizon, the ever returning welcome of the seasons, the family.

Rings are always there, like "Heaven." When an under–six–year–old tiptoes around the outside of a circle, as in "A Tisket, A Tasket," watch the little face. Where is that child that she or he feels so happy again? What secret place has been reached? Is the child a "simple-minded" being, enjoying merely "simple-minded" things? Or was the poet Wordsworth accurate when he described the child as "trailing clouds of glory"? Does the little one still live in a world we cannot any longer get back to ourselves?

Obviously, yes. And yet most of us remember a time, however vaguely, which was much different from our present state — a time which was "heavenly." The world seemed soft, gentle, cloudlike, friendly, malleable. We were protected by a sheath of well-being. Children live easily in that glory–filled world. Watch when they fall on the ground. Their shrieks are out of all proportion to the damage done. It is because the little ones have been shocked out of an enveloping cloud of light into a sudden realization of the solidity of the earth. The soul resents this. When you ritualize this cosmic happening in the garment of a game, such as the lovely "Ring Around the Roses," you lead children lovingly, gently down to earth, and they begin to enjoy the fun of it. They feel the welcome. Bit by bit they don't mind staying. If we manage this with loving concern, then that heavenly, strengthening, magical, self-creating place will remain with each child for the rest of their lives.

## The Forces of Play

The forces of play are those which the body uses for healthy growth, uprightness, integrity, gracefulness, and self-control. Later these will be internalized in their turn to become the mature person's mode of moral perception. Games strengthen and smooth each child's characteristic way of interacting with their worlds.

There is no need to over-emphasize the differences between work and play, as if one were desirable and one unpleasant. The child is absorbing all the gestures and attitudes of the adult with wonder and reverence. If you do not give it cause to feel otherwise, the child will love you and wish to be like you. It is worth making all gestures lovely and purposeful, even if it is only washing hands or sweeping floors. For that is one more truly wonderful thing about little children. They give you a second chance at magic.

When growth forces become congested through lack of play, they injure a child. Fear and fussiness develop. Freely offered willingness is replaced by dull obedience. Play, ranging from simple goofing-off to the most complex of formal games, is children's form of love and duty. When a child says: "I can't, I'm playing," the adult does not have to be offended.

## Interruptions and Completions

Nor should there be any need to interrupt unless something is particularly urgent. To "think ahead" is something the adult might do more usefully than a child, who is wrapped in timelessness while immersed in an absorbing activity. Remember that childrens' attention span is very short. One can easily let the game play itself out, or each have a turn, or let it happen "one more time." Then the child does not face the next activity in a surly manner. It's the kind of "discipline" that works.

If one feels that the imaginative play is getting out of hand, or that the play is not being imaginative enough, then is when the adult's participation can come to the rescue. For instance, if the child is a pirate, sailing the seven seas on your best couch, you can make him or her captain of another ship (one more to your liking) and offer the old raincoat for sail, explaining that it is stronger in a tempest than your best shawl. One appears in the child's dream only momentarily. The child will understand what the purpose is, but will not have been disturbed in the full, imaginative completion of the play. Completion itself is a virtue in playing games. Even though children do not experience time in the same way as adults, it is helpful for you to think of a child's game as having a beginning, middle, and end. If you want children to grow up and be able to accomplish a set task, it does no good to break their inclination to complete their own activities. These activities may reach and form firmer habit patterns than merely responding to adult orders will ever do. To let them complete an act out of joy is to strengthen their resolve. It will firm their ability to go through to an end. Completion serves its own purpose. To force children against their will weakens their courage and their ability to act independently. By breaking their will, one tends to create rigid, fearful, selfish, or apathetic adults.

## WHERE TO PLAY

Ring games are perhaps the earliest of all. They are joyful, simple, and yet they have a ritual aspect as well. One can find room to play them almost anywhere: in classrooms, apartments, gardens, playgrounds. However, there are certain forms to all games which need to be maintained. Once you know these inner forms, then you might make up your own games at any time. You may sometimes change the words, although this must be done with great sensitivity and care.

## *RING AROUND THE ROSES*

> Ring Around the Roses
> Pocket full of Poses
> Ashes, ashes,
> We all fall down
> The cows are in the meadow
> Lying fast asleep
> Ashes, ashes
> We all get up again.

### How to Play the Game

The children hold hands and skip in a circle. On the last line of the first verse, they "all fall down," letting go of each other as they fall. They stay down chanting the second verse, and all get up again on its last line. Taking hands they skip around in a circle again.

It is the simplest of all games, reflecting the simplest of all truths.

### What to Know and What to Tell the Children

Children love to "fall from heaven" in a loving situation, as on a rug, sand, or grass. Watch them holding hands and tumbling down. They look at each other with an amused kind of recognition, as if they remembered each other from somewhere else and had not just been all together standing up.

We need not talk to children about such things. That would make them self-conscious. However, the imagery  behind this particular game harks back to very ancient beliefs. The roots of roses are gnarled and bark-like. The stems have thorns. They even contain a small poison. This prickly state is overcome by the beautiful blossom, which not only fills the garden with a wonderful scent, but also creates the healing rosehip berry once the petals fall. In the game, "Ring Around the Roses," is the ring of little humans not yet separated or overwhelmed by earth forces. When the children fall down, they bump into matter, earth. That is the first verse. It jibes with their experience. By taking hands in the second verse, they express what happens in daily life: one can overcome the hard, prickly nature of earth experience and blossom beneficially, like the rose. It's just that one has to do something about it.

No one ever falls up.

*SALLY GO ROUND THE SUN*
 Sally go round the Sun.
 Sally go round the Moon.
 Sally go round the chimney pots
 On a Saturday afternoon.


## How to Play the Game

The children form themselves into a ring without holding hands. Check their toes and shoulders to help them towards a fine circle shape. (If you have some invisible magic powder in your pocket, it sometimes helps to sprinkle it on toes that are too far out or too far in. Without even a word, it's astonishing how a small sprinkle awakens little people if done with a sense of magic). When the third line is reached, the children turn around each on their own spot; then on the fourth line each settles back into the circle.

That is all. But that is everything  Within this simplicity, there are magnificent overtones – at first the planetary element of Sun and Moon, then the floating down to earth while turning in a cosmic spiral, finally the settling into the individual self within time.

Before the planets Pluto and Uranus were discovered, the planet Saturn was said to course the outermost planetary ring of our solar system. Since ancient days, Saturn (often called the Ancient of Days) was seen as the planet which influences personal destiny. It was said that under the guidance of Saturn, people were forced to come to grips with the most difficult aspects of their lives. So said the tradition. Notice how the detail of the day, Saturn's day, "on a Saturday afternoon," rolls so deliciously off the tongue, and has such unsuspected resonance.

## A SUGGESTION

Given the simplicity of this game, you can see why the mood you create as you play will mean so much. Solemnity is often as magical an element as fun or rough-house. You can choose the mood you find appropriate to your situation. The sense of wonder is what you seek.

As guides, we try to lead the little ones in a kindly, non-coercive way. We know that their lives will not be any easier than our own. Even so, there is no need to toughen them so they miss out on the gentle, loving, fun qualities of life — those qualities that create wonder, laughter, and confidence without competition. What we wish is to help them grow strong, so they will be able to overcome any obstructions their destinies hold for them

- strong enough to remain gentle and loving, non-blaming, productive and creative in the face of any hindrances they may find in their paths.

As you create a circle, always form a very round one. The children thus bring their individual selves into harmonious relationship with the group. Without tactful guidance, one child will jump too far into the center, a shyer one will stay too far outside. Some will try to crowd together, others to keep too far apart. As they practice getting their toes and shoulders into a perfect round, they learn to take harmonious control of their own bodies. They also learn to enhance the group. The trick is to allow the children to find their way into this perfect ring in perfect freedom. It should be their own individuality that leads them to create the circle along with the others. No one, neither child nor adult, should lose either his/her individuality or his/her freedom when he/she cooperates with others.

*LOOBY LOO*

Here we go Looby Loo
Here we go Looby Light
Here we go Looby Loo
All on a Saturday night.

I put my right hand in
I put my right hand out,
I give my hand a shake, shake, shake,
And turn myself about.

*Additional verses*:

I put my left hand in, etc.
I put my left foot in, etc.
I put my right foot in, etc.
I put  my whole self in, etc.

## How to Play the Game

The children form a circle. In this case they do not hold hands. First they sing the chorus, and as they do, they follow the chanted directions that change with each verse.

## A Suggestion

We advance another step with this game. Although the children still partake of the anonymity of the eternal round, they stand upright and begin to find their place on earth through directions in space. They learn to listen, because the words change with each verse. We still leave the little ones in the golden warmth of childhood, and yet we recognize that the incarnating spirit is coming into life at a specific point in time, and at a certain place on the globe. We do not emphasize this, since children do not fit too snugly into their bodies and do not consciously orient themselves in space or time until much later. Merely to have them in your adult consciousness, however, will strengthen the child's relation to the deeper impulses underlying the play.

This act of regularly keeping them in your consciousness is neither magical nor particularly mysterious. It means you will be firmly attentive to them when you interact, and they will respond accordingly.

To orient oneself in space is to experience the earth. When taking hold of space, children first stand upright, next they find their balance, then they take their first step on our little  planet. Later, these acts will be internalized into virtues. To be upright, to be harmonously balanced, to be purposefully self-directed, are characteristic qualities of the ennobled human being.

## IMITATION

From earliest years, see if you can get your children to follow your gestures, and to imitate the way you speak the words of the song without your having to tell them to do so. It might take a little longer, at first, but it will be worth it. It promotes initiative in the gentlest way. At this stage children are primarily imitating the adult. Prove it for yourself. Sit down on the floor and draw circles with your finger. See how long the two year old child can resist drawing a circle on the floor. Imitation, when offered out of the child's own initiative, helps him learn to act out of his own free will. When you watch this process happen over time, you will be glad you did not badger your children with unnecessary orders and explanations.

*HERE WE GO ROUND THE MULBERRY BUSH*

*Chorus*

Here we go round the mulberry bush,
The mulberry bush, the mulberry bush.
Here we go round the mulberry bush
On a cold and frosty morning.

*Verses:*
1. This is the way we wash our clothes, etc.
   So early Monday morning.
2. This is the way we iron our clothes, etc.
   So early Tuesday morning.
3. This is the way we scrub our floors, etc.
   So early Wednesday morning.
4. This is the way we mend our clothes, etc.
   So early Thursday morning.
5. This is the way we sweep the house, etc.
   So early Friday morning.
6. This is the way we bake our bread, etc.
   So early Saturday morning.
7. Then we play when work is done, etc.
   So early Sunday morning.

## How to Play the Game

First the children form a ring. They then skip around in the circle, ever alert to maintaining its shape. As they skip, they sing the chorus: "Here we go round the Mulberry bush ..." At the end of the verse, they stop, still protective of their circle. They then begin to sing the first verse, demonstrating in gestures how to "wash our clothes." Then they circle once again, holding hands, singing the chorus once again. The children alternate each verse with chorus up to verse six. They then skip in a circle for verse seven to show how we play when work is done.

## Variations

Mulberry can be varied as time passes. Once the children know the words, then in one verse you can all pretend to be giants washing giant clothes, next little raindrop fairies washing little fairy things. Lead the voices so they get very loud and deep, or very tiny and high, for the occasion. Gestures also change accordingly: large arm movements for the giants, tiny finger and hand movements for the little fairies. Always restore the balance with the middle ground of the human scale.

The children may also circle without holding hands, although the circle still needs to be preserved as perfectly as possible. They may go fast, faster, then slow down to a snail's pace. They can take large steps, and then change down to teeny ones, returning in each game to the balanced human tread. It is with attention to these details that the educational value of games surfaces. Your skillful, kindly consideration in a loving atmosphere will become a reliable source of strength for these children when they are adults themselves.

In this way you familiarize the youngsters with the realities of size, as they learn to control their own hands and feet. You familiarize them with the effects of sound, particularly their own voices, through the use of loudness and softness. You help them to be aware of their own characteristic body speeds. There are slow children with vague movements; boisterous one with big gestures; ones with quick, unpredictable motions; others with elegant, but self-absorbed rhythms. You do not wish to change a child's characteristic speed. Rather you want to put it within each one's own power. In that way they will be free to choose when to work together and when to work alone. You try to reach their individual speeds without coercion and without harm, through these simple and fun changes in the game.

You see, to prepare a child to write, we first teach him or her to listen. To prepare a child to read, we help him or her to speak clearly. The powers of transformation inherent in a child's very being are working with us. None of us are alone in rearing a child. Nature is on our side, and human nature, too. Much of the time we just do not give these helping factors a chance to help us. We interfere and block the workings of miraculous processes.

In "Mulberry" the adult world is celebrated in its most revered form: the daily life. By four years, and sometimes even younger, children have begun to attach their longings to the earth and to the actions they observe adults perform. It is one reason why we should attempt to keep our gestures gentle, precise, and fully formed– in other words, always worthy of imitation. If none of the actions in the game is done in the home because of mechanical aids, then choose some useful actions that are done by hand: washing faces, brushing hair, sweeping, raking. It is not desirable to select mechanical actions. A human behaves out of a different impulse than a machine, and this difference is of the utmost importance when you stand before a young child.

The forces of play are those which the body uses for healthy growth, for uprightness, integrity, gracefulness, and self-control. Later these will be internalized in their turn to become the mature person's mode of moral perception. Games strengthen and smooth each child's characteristic way of interacting with their worlds.

## SUGGESTIONS

As you learn to play with little children, you will be less self-conscious when you do not have other adults just watching. Children have complete belief and trust in you in the first place, so self-consciousness conveys a puzzling sense of your inadequacy. It is one mood you wish to avoid at all cost. It casts soul doubt.

Another thing to watch out for is how you speak to children. Rather than telling the children what to do, try to reach a mood of "Let's Pretend." Pretend to be giants. Pretend to be tiny fairies, because you want children to have strong, individualized wills. People obey orders, but each time they do so against their own will, they are weakened slightly. Your clear speech and well-formed gestures will affect their gestures in a way more kindly and deeply than reprimands.

## A Word About Chants

Sometimes we read a nursery rhyme, and it seems quite frightening. This is generally because it has been taken out of the context of a game, and, therefore, lost its beneficial power. Unless you can find your way back to the meaning of a rhyme, it is best to leave it out altogether. Usually it can be related back to a daily activity, and then one finds that the words activate a child's movements in a perfectly harmless way. For instance:

> *DAVY DAVY DUMPLING*
> Davy, Davy, Dumpling
> Boil him in a pot
> Sugar him, and butter him
> And eat him while he's hot.

Said by itself, this has unpleasant overtones. Said while making dumplings (or doughnuts or cookies), this has another tone altogether.

Or take the wonderful *A TISKET, A TASKET*:

## A TISKET, A TASKET

> A Tisket, a Tasket,
> A green and yellow basket,
> I sent a letter to my love,
> And on the way I dropped it,
> I dropped it,
> I dropped it,
> My green and yellow basket.
> If somebody picks it up,
> I think that I will die.

In A Tisket, A Tasket, the last word of the last line seems extreme. However, we find the reason for the sudden shock when we analyze the game itself.

### How to Play the Game

In "A Tisket A Tasket " the children sit on the floor in a circle. This is still the ever encircling planetary rounds, the earthly globe, the protective rounds of nature, daily life, friends. One child is then chosen to skip around the outside of the circle. This child holds a handkerchief in his or her hand. We reach back here to original language: the language of gesture. It is the language that nature herself uses, which is the first "writing" we ever learn. Everyone sings the song. All the children listen attentively, because at the phrase "I think that I will die," the circling child will drop the handkerchief behind the back of one of the sitting children.

The one child that must notice the handkerchief, who must take immediate action, is the one child who cannot directly see the action. It happens behind her back. She must read the faces of her friends or notice the running child's empty hands. Then she must confirm her suspicions by looking behind her to make sure the handkerchief is there. Once she confirms that she has indeed been chosen, she jumps up and tries to catch the first child before he reaches round the circle to the empty place.

Unless he is too distracted by the excitement, the first child usually reaches the empty place safely. There he "dies", that is, he merges back into the protective anonymity of the circle. Another now takes the riskier path of individuality. With handkerchief in hand she begins to tiptoe around the circle to the chanting of the sitting children.

### THE FARMER'S IN THE DELL
Chorus:
> The Farmer's in the Dell
> The Farmer's in the Dell
> Hi Ho the Derry o,
> The Farmer's in the Dell.

Verses:
> The Farmer takes a Wife, etc.
> The Wife takes a Child, etc.
> The Child takes a Cow, etc.
> The Cow takes a Dog, etc.
> The Dog takes a Cat, etc.
> The Cat takes a Rat, etc.
> The Rat takes a Cheese, etc.

## How to Play the Game

One child is chosen from among volunteers to be "Farmer" and stands in the middle while the others hold hands and skip around in a circle, singing the chorus and first verse. The children stop as the Farmer chooses a "Wife" from the ring, and then they skip around again singing the chorus and second verse. The "Wife" chooses a "Child" from the ring. This pattern continues until all the children have been chosen, including the "Cheese," and all the verses have been sung. The one chosen in each subsequent verse is the one who chooses the next person to step into the center.

Repeat the chorus between each verse. When everyone is in the center, then all except the "Cheese" run back to the circle and skip around chanting "The Cheese stands alone", etc. After a final chorus, the "Cheese" becomes the "Farmer," and so the great, ever-repeating rounds, now including the individualized being, continue on their familiar and welcome way.

## A Thought

This game contains one of the most poignant moments in all childhood: the moment at the end when everyone returns to the circle and the "Cheese stands alone." Happily the child who is Cheese will be Farmer in the next round, but for the moment it has a profound and oftentimes unsettling effect to be standing alone at the end of the game with everyone staring at you.

At the beginning of any enterprise there spreads before one a variety of possibilities, opportunities, and hope. At the end, something is fixed. You stand alone with your achievement. It is a sudden shock to experience this moment when one appears to be deserted, but observed, unable to hide. This experience will be repeated over and over again throughout one's life. Therefore, it is just this kind of game which most requires adult tact and kindness. How and when it is introduced will make a great difference. And just when a little one is chosen to be Cheese should be considered very carefully. One should probably already be five or six years old. Even so, many five and six- year-olds simply collapse in tears at the premature loneliness of it all. Some people remember this moment when they are fifty and sixty.

What the adult does in sensitive times of this sort will afffect the child deeply, perhaps for the rest of his or her life. Do not rush this experience. If you can, alert yourself to certain happenings inside the child. Sense the crucial moment when she or he innocently touches the earth and stays. It is a tremendous event. Do not precipitate it and lose the opportunity for the healthy experience. Externalizing this moment so fraught with fate in the game "Farmer" is a true celebration.

## CHOICES

Some games are quiet, some move in predestined forms, while others partake of as much movement as possible within the limits of self-control. Energetic, graceful, happy movement which is not boisterous or out-of-control is to be encouraged. If a game loses form because a child gets too wild, bring the children back into a circle and lead the game into very slow movements. Children can be just as intrigued by a slow rhythm as by a fast one. By getting the children back into the rhythmic element of the game, you get them back in control and this gives them a chance to get themselves under their own control. Through these gentle games, children have found themselves on earth, have located themselves in space, have learned to listen, to act in the moment, to individualize out of the anonymity of the circle. Now there is something new: there are things to get done, missions to accomplish, causes to uphold, duties to be faced. There are all the complexities of daily life to which one brings one's own moral nature. How will we behave, how should we behave, in order to accomplish the tasks life sets in our way? Some people think they have the answers. Others think there are no answers. We offer our children the strength to find their own ways, in freedom – not alone, but on their own.

## ORANGES AND LEMONS

Oranges & lemons say the Bells of St. Clemens,
Pancakes and fritters say the Bells of St. Peter's.
Chip, chop, chip, chop, chop chop chop
Here comes a candle to light you to bed,
Here comes a chopper to chop off your head.

*Verses:*
Two sticks and an apple, say the bells of Whitechapel,
Pokers and pans, say the Bells of St. Anne's.
Etc.

### How to Play the Game

Two children stand face to face. These are the Orange and the Lemon. They raise their arms over their heads and then take each other's hands to make a bridge. The other children parade around in a circle. When they get to the "chip, chop" verse, the Orange and Lemon pretend to catch those going under their

51

bridge. Lithe arms touch the others for a fleeting moment, but then let them flutter away, like butterflies. Not until the final verse is anyone actually "caught."

> Here comes a candle to light you to bed
> *Here comes a chopper to chop off your head.*

Once caught in the arms of the" Lemon and Orange," each child must choose which he wishes to become, and then goes to stand behind one or other of the bridge children. The chant begins to make a new kind of sense. Its apparently macabre note is belied by the choice. A deeply felt internal happening is externalized in the ritual of this game.

Prior to this event, thoughts have touched the little beings lightly, swiftly, much as the little arms of the two bridge children touched the heads of the paraders in the game. In the end, though the moment comes when thoughts take hold. The head is "separated" from the unconscious workings of the body. The child begins to think in logical ways. Energies, which up until then have been used to form the whole body, head included, separate off and begin to tug at consciousness.

The change is signaled by the loss of baby teeth – a spectacular outward show of an otherwise hidden event. Most of us can remember back to this moment when bit by bit we become aware of our surroundings; events disengaged themselves from the general blur of childhood and began to form clear pictures, many of which we still retain as memory images. This took place around six or seven years, although it varies considerably from person to person. It is a fateful moment, still mostly ignored in our time. The game ritualizes and celebrates this event. It is resolved in a grand tug of war between "Oranges" and "Lemons." The heavenly ring is almost forgotten. It has been transformed by experience on earth.

Once upon a time, we belonged without barriers or borders. Then we separated out into tribes and races, nations and religions. We began the long journey into our own individuality. We now begin to experience the individuality of others around us. What we do about this will be a matter of concern all our lives.

Today, we can easily find a variety of games in toy shops and libraries. You will soon be able to sense how they repeat the same incarnating steps in wonderful new ways. Still I think sometimes that there is a need for one other game which I hope will be invented someday soon – a game in which we do not choose merely to "be ourselves" nor to "possess another," but a game in which we awaken instead to the other's full experience, as well as our own. It will be a game for all people, individuals among individuals. It will create a new kind of "ring," and a new kind of "heaven" – a heaven on earth.

# SEED GAMES

When we are born, everyone knows we are staying as soon as we take our first breath. The last thing we do in life is breathe out. Then everyone knows we have left. In between, lungs, heart, and all life-experience see-saw in the harmonizing play between the forces of contraction and expansion.

Is it an exaggeration to say that this accordion-like force is the characteristic experience of life on earth? Imagine light and darkness, winter and summer, day and night. Think of breathing in and out every minute of your life. Think of the need to be oneself, and the need to understand others. Remember joy and sorrow.

I think that the most astonishing example is water. Water molecules expand and move to become steam. When they crowd together in an ever smaller space, they form ice. In between, water is life sustaining .

So?

No, that is not the dazzling surprise. This is it: When water cools, it contracts, and as it cools further, it contracts more firmly, just as everything does. Water turns to mush, then to thin ice, then to thick, hard crust. In a good cold winter, full bottles explode, lakes and rivers freeze over. In an ice age, glaciers rise high into the sky.

Rise into the sky?

Why don't they sink to the bottom of the deepest ocean?

Usually when anything contracts, it gets heavier since it is now all in one ever-smaller place. So why don't the glaciers just sink like everything else? I mean everything else.

What happens is that water in the process of turning to ice, contracts until it reaches 0 degrees centigrade. If it kept on going, and nothing ever stopped its contracting, all life on earth would end. Instead, it jumps for joy.

54

Well, that is a poetic expression. What happens is that the newly-formed ice suddenly expands. If it didn't, there probably would not have been any life on earth. The ice expands, floats on top of the oceans, lakes, rivers, ponds, and puddles, where it forms protective coats which keep the remaining warmth of the deeper waters from escaping. The colder it gets, the more protection the warmer waters need, so the thicker the overcoats of ice become. What this means is that from the tiniest, most intricate algae, to the most magnificent of mammals, life has been maintained in the water's depths. Water expands to form ice. This oddly protective behaviour not only breaks bottles on a cold winter's night but guarantees that life on our globe will survive.

Water expands into protective gasses and contracts until it forms ice. In between, human life can flourish.

What else expands and contracts as regularly as heart, breath, and water do? Visualize an acorn expanding into a magnificent oak tree, then producing acorns anew, acorns which are really contracted oaks. Visualize any seed, from peas to pomegranates, from parsley to pumpkins. They all expand into fully formed plants, then contract into the tiniest area once again, there to produce another seed, another plant, and repeat the cycle over again. Animals do the same with their seeds.

Scientists say our universe exploded from a three-second "Big Bang". Ancient traditions relate that before a "Big Bang" there was a rest period where nothing was manifest. Tradition maintains that these two states have followed each other like pumpkin seed and pumpkin, over and over again, with one important difference: our universe is on a spiral, repeating, yes, but moving along at the same time.

Do humans perhaps do the same on repeating turns of the spiral, in life, in death?

Few of us know for sure.

When we work with our littlest children, a great many mysteries hover around us — like angels. Then, when we feel inadequate, reverence and wonder are our best guides.

No need to make up your mind as if it were a rumpled bed. Leave it open. The sense of wonder awakens us to mysteries. Knowledge contracts us into facts. Children will need both throughout their lives. As their first guides we do our best to keep their sense of wonder intact for as long as it is within our power to do so. Cold facts will rain in on them soon enough — that is not the problem. Will they understand the facts? Will the "fact" be found incorrrect later and meantime stop the children from thinking warm-heartedly?

Seed games protect children from the beartrap of "either-or" thinking where our choices are either "this" or "that". When we play with the pulsing forces of expansion and contraction, we do not choose sides for our little ones, but try, instead, to understand how opposites can be reconciled. The only place we can be sure about is in human experience.

## ASPECTS OF SEED GAMES

For some years children seem to pulse between earth and heaven. You watch them sleep and wake, daydream and observe, wonder and remember, explode in laughter, and collapse in tears. Pulsing like strange underwater sea creatures in unknown ocean currents, they open wide to their universe and contract into their earth-bound selves.

With seed games we guide children into one of the most characteristic experiences of our sojourn on earth: the accordion-like, pulsing experience of contraction-expansion. In the process we help them harmonize their breathing, strengthen their heart systems, stretch their imaginations, and achieve some under-standing of how their inner and outer worlds mix, meet, and merge. We assist them to balance the pull of their inner 'I' against the pull of the world. Then when you feel their pulse, it will be beating in synchronicity with some of the most mysterious rhythms of the world.

## SPRINGTIME SEEDS

### How to Play the Game

Stand in a circle. Hold hands. Check that toes, and shoulders try to make a circle. Drop hands and start the chant:

> We are little flowers in bud
> The Sun comes to warm us
> Up sleepy heads
> Open your petals wide.

On the first line everyone crouches down on the floor, bodies curled and fingers clenched. On the second, when the sun warms, heads slowly rise.

On the third line the children begin to stand up, and on the last line they are up in a circle, arms opened wide, fingers wiggling wide to the world.

Can you imagine how you would play this game in the fall?

### Where To Play the Game

Any small area will do: living room, garden, playroom. And any number can play. If there are only one or two children present, you can play this game quietly on an airplane, train, in a hotel room, or in any cramped space where some exercise is in order.

Later, when you go for a walk, look for snowdrops, crocuses, cyclamen, and other springtime flowers — even if you have to find them in the flowershops. Seamlessly, you extend the game into real life.

## The Uses of Story

In this springtime game children imitate and empathize with the growth forces of the plant world. You see how an imaginative picture leads to action in a very spontaneous way. This pulsing connection between imagination and action is what we seek to use in our daily dealings with our children. Artistically achieved, this will leave them free, their soul stuff undamaged. As adults they will be better able to choose to work with, or to withstand, the coercions of the practical world.

We use story to instigate action, because orders compel children, leaving no room for their own initiatives. Sometimes we need a child to do what we want, but even then we try to help them meet our request out of their own freely offered will. This is what we aim for. We don't merely abandon them into freedom with questions such as: "What do you want? What do you like?" We also guide, inform, mentor, and ally ourselves with them, making sense of choices, so consequences don't get out of hand. It is no use to let children be free to choose, if you do not give them some means to evaluate their choices. Ultimately, we do not wish to tell them what to think or how to feel or act. We wish to guide them to make their own choices, freely, with us but belonging to their world, too. We want our children to have skills to make courageous and morally-informed choices: to take part in the enterprises of their generation — a future they can sense but which is unknown to us.

## INDIVIDUALIZING

Children enter the earth experience in a new way when they are about three years old. They walk and run rather well, speak fairly clearly, and already think in rudimentary ways. Their sense of wonder leads them to explore, then to remember and talk about what they have found out. Usually in the third year of life, a child begins differentiating out from the pulsating universe. In a dramatic, yet still ephemeral manner, children begin to use that most mysterious expression of all: I am, thereby acknowledging the seed of their own individuality. They no longer feel totally merged with the bubbling cauldron of the world. They notice that the cat has feelings, and they may refrain from stepping on its tail. They notice that the table does not, and, may stop kicking it when bumped.

It is a special time, one of the great milestone moments in life. Francis Edmunds, founder of Emerson College in England, which is famous for its Waldorf Teachers Training Course, once described it to me this way: his grandchild was standing at the top of the stairs. "I am going to fall down," the boy called to his grandfather waiting at the bottom. "I should have felt fear for his safety," Edmunds related ruefully. "Instead, I heard his first 'I am' and fell to my knees in reverence at the mighty event which had taken place before my eyes."

*EE - AH - 0*

### How to Play the Game

Children stand in a circle holding hands. Once everyone is ready to begin, the children drop their hands to their sides. They chant the verses and mime the gestures. That is all.

> How tall are we?
> As tall as a tree.
>
> Can we go far?
> Yes, to a star.
>
> How do we go?
> Round as an 'O'.

> O away
> Ah away
> EE away

As you begin the chant, heads loosely fall onto chests, relaxed. Then on the second line of the first verse, the children stand as tall and straight as they can: Feet are together, and hands by their sides. Each forms an I. They are on solid ground.

On the second line of the second verse the children lift their arms wide, and jump open their legs. They form a star. There is a part of them which will reach for the stars.

On the third verse, they form a large O with their arms and fingers. How will they go to their star? With loving empathy.

Next lead the children backwards as you say:

"O away", drop hands to the sides.
"Ah away", jump feet together
"Ee away", relax your stance, drop head onto chest.

Repeat the game three or four times, getting faster as you do it, then slowing down again to bring the children back into a normal rhythm. Vary the speed from day to day, depending on the moods of the children, the weather, the seasons.

However, no matter how fast you lead them, you, the adult, say the words and make the gestures clearly enough so everyone can follow easily all the time. Don't explain and don't expect the children to say the words by themselves for awhile. That's all right, though, because it's the gestures that count. And repetition will work eventually.

Body language is the first language children learn. All the later languages are mere abstractions of this very first one. When you look at the sky to see if the storm is coming, you read the body language of our globe. Imitate the world as you introduce your children into it. Make your acts and your gestures meaningful, graceful, generous. Then let the children imitate you. Children absorb the action of others. Make yourself worthy of their imitation. Thoughts and feelings are expressed in gestures whether you know it or not. A child learns to read your body language right from the start. Lips tight with anger, fists clenched, restless pacing, fearful looks, all speak clearly to the youngster. When your gestures are loving and fun-filled, and the youngsters know what to expect, then they will be happy to imitate you. The capacity for imitation in one to six-year-olds creates a mood of reverence and initiative. Both are virtues which lead to personal integrity and personal freedom

## THE HOUSE

### How to Play the Game

Stand in a circle holding hands. Drop hands as you chant:

"We are going into a little house on the edge of the Fairy Wood." Keep the circle crisp and well formed.
"Let us open the door."
Everyone jumps feet apart.
"Now we are inside. We close the door."
Jump feet together. Check that circle remains crisp. Everyone stands straight and still.
"We forgot our dog. Open the door."
Jump feet apart.
"Close the door quickly. Lets go upstairs."
Feet together. Pretend to stomp upstairs while remaining in place.
"The sun is shining. Open the windows."
Make a big O with the arms above your head.
"A cloud is passing. It's going to rain. Let's close the windows."

A full curve of the arms back down to the sides. "Windows" and "doors" both closed. Now, tiptoe up another flight of stairs to the attic where there are more windows, but very little ones, for little elves.

"The storm has passed. Let's open the little windows and let out the elves."

This time, since the windows are small, we use only the hands and fingers. Check your circle. Put fingertips of pointers and thumbs together and hold up in front of your face. Repeat the process watching that feet are together, gestures clear.

"Close it for the day."
"Open it so the elf can come back for the night."
"Close it for the night."

Each time raise hands up in front of the face, then bring back down to the sides as the windows close. Then tiptoe down the pretend stairs, and open and close the big windows on the second floor a few times. Then stomp down to the ground floor and out the front door. Remember to open and close the door by jumping your feet together as you go out.

With the simplest of visual imaginations you have brought the arms and legs, hands and feet, fingers and toes in play in complex ways.

When you vary the tempo you will engage the children's will. Get them to open and close their windows very fast as pretend storms come and go. Move slowly as the storms pass by.

People your house with your own creatures: have giants on the ground floor, people on the middle one, and tiny elves on top. Or different kinds of animals: small and large, fast and slow.

When the windows are tiny, and only the tiny hands are used, make your voice soft as a whisper, and high. When the

63

doors are big and heavy, make your voice low and loud. Stomp on the groundfloor and tiptoe in the attic. The variety amuses children getting them to pay attention,. They then imitate you easily, out of their own free will — and with a sense of fun.

## A Final Thought

Speech reaches a person where damage of a permanent nature can be done. Even the bones heal and one walks as good as new. But thoughtless adult talk which tears at the fabric of truth from which a child gains confidence in the world may inflict wounds that never heal.

That's why we should both think and feel our way into the situation before speaking roughly to a child. For instance, should one wish to say: "Stop playing around!," stop first and see what the child is really up to. Will you interrupt some important impulse:

> to concentrate,
> to act independently,
> to work with others,
> to be depended upon?

Consider what you are interrupting.

# SPIRAL GAMES

When we shape a spiral, we are repeating the expansion-contraction gesture of the universe. Hard-edged and tight are experienced in a safe situation and found to be very different from diffuse and airy. As you play the games, you will soon see how these extremes attract different children. Your goal will be to bring a human balance between the two opposites. As we thought in the beginning, human experience is a place where opposites reconcile.

It will be fairly difficult for some youngsters to keep their spirals evenly spaced at first. The quiet, the deferential, or intimidated, will tend to make them too small, while the boisterous, thoughtless, or hyper will make them too large. The circle, too, will tend to break when the children run for joy. There will always be some who get too easily outside themselves and roughhouse hard. Certain children will tend to lose the form of the game sooner than others. And at first, children who have never played these spiral games will have trouble. Even so, how soon children learn to play with accuracy will depend more on their character and temperament than on their skills.

As their loving guide, watch for these tendencies. Then as ally (rather than boss) tactfully help get these personal characteristics under each child's own control.

Careful perceptions on your part will lead you into new understandings of the children in your care. You'll worry and fuss less. Sometimes a child who always breaks up the circle by running too fast will take responsibility for the shape if made leader. Sometimes a deferential, cry-baby child, who always makes the circle too cramped, will take responsibility when gently encouraged to sit in the center, the object of all the attention. Or do the reverse on another occasion. The shy child may dread the center. Don't push or insist. Merely note the fact for another occasion and then encourage the child another way. Bit by bit the timid will gain confidence, and the overly boisterous will achieve gentleness. Thus, they'll be able to use their characteristic approaches to the world in ways which are less likely to hamper their own efforts. It is not that we wish to make all children alike, but that by noticing their basic temperamental differences, we may help them attain ease in their selves, their bodies, and their environments.

## *BIRTHDAY CHILD*

### How to Play the Game
The Birthday Child sits in the middle of the room. Ask the other children to bring a gift. The present is pretend, but each child carries it as if it were real. That is they show by their gestures whether it is heavy, tiny, wiggly, outsized. They whisper to you what it is before they enter the spiral. Then the children line up, and you, or a chosen child, leads the others round in a generous spiral to greet the Birthday Child at the center. The children offer their gifts with pomp and ceremony, each one waiting for the Birthday Child to unwrap it before telling what they have brought. While some children are still coming in, the leader takes the children out in a clearly visualized spiral, making sure as they spiral out that they do not bump into the children spiraling in. Once out, they form a circle around the Birthday Child. Everyone follows round in a clear circle, arms raised high, fingers wiggling cheerfully. Go very fast, then bit by bit slow down and come to a stop in a well-formed circle.

Be artistic when you play this game. Remember the presents each child is bringing, so you can say something imaginative on occasion, like, "the pot of gold is tipping, Jerry, hold it straight."

If you like you can make up a poem to go with the walk, or sing a song like Happy Birthday. Nowadays, people are so inventive that one cannot help but be happy. They dare to bring gentle, thoughtful , fun, and seasonal creations in poetry or music to share with their little ones. Once you start, ideas spring up like flowers in springtime.

### GNOMES' HOME

Through echoing caverns we run and glide.
Through cracks in the rocks we slip and slide.
 Over great boulders we leap and bound,
Our small candle lamps show when treasure is found.
We hammer, we hammer from morning till night.
We hammer together the treasure so bright.
 Now filling our sacks with the fruits of our work;
We heave and haul, and tug and jerk,
 Until we are out in the light above
Our treasure a gift for the friends we love.

### How to Play the Game

This game repeats the archetypal pattern of all spiral games. From it you can learn to invent your own. Start by standing straight in a circle. One child then leads the others in a spiral to the center. They begin by standing in a circle. First they walk around the circle, then they enter the spiral path, crouching farther and farther down as they proceed into the imagined dark. Chanting as they go, they act out the words. Gnome's hammer as they spiral in; then when they lift their heavy sacks and prepare to spiral out, they start by crouching but slowly unwind until they are standing up in the circle once again. They run in a ring, slowly at first then fast, faster, then back to slow. They learn to stop in a perfectly formed circle, toes and shoulders forming the round, too.

At first in any game, one child will go too slow, another too fast, a third will push and stumble, a fourth will talk and distract. However, we know that the shy child, the clever one, the deferring, the overbearing, the quiet, and the loud — each one longs for balance. So we do not downgrade nor weaken any child's distinctive qualities. Without squashing anything, we help them get themselves within their own self-control. The same opportunity to lead or be last will reach each child for different reasons. As their ally, you treat each one fairly, tactfully, always with a sense of fun, never mechanically.

*SNAIL'S HOUSE*

### How to Play the Game

This game takes the same form as the Birthday or Gnome's Game. However, the child at the center chooses to be an animal, perhaps a quiet one, like Mr. Snail. This animal lives at the center of a spiral. Other pretend animal friends spiral in one by one for a visit to Snail. As they go they chant:

We will pay a little visit to the curly house of Snail.
Round and round until we find him in his little house so frail.
Then we turn to go back homeward, awinding all the way,
Till we come out from our tunnel to the sunny light of day.

The children crouch down as they walk in the spiral, and bit by bit rise up as they walk out. It is as if the snail house were getting smaller and smaller as it would in real life. Each one makes noises appropriate to his or her chosen animal. What does an elephant say to a snail? Listen to your little ones and find out. Then lead the children out in a spiral, walking faster as you go, straightening up bit by bit. With care run into a well-formed circle, keeping up on tiptoes, chest full, everything expanded to its outermost edges. Try to keep the circle. Raise hands up in the air, wiggle fingers freely. Slow down to a walk and then stop in a well-formed circle. Toes and shoulders form the rounds, not just tummies.

### Your Own Spiral Game

Having traveled the whole world over, I have been impressed with the variety of celebrations which take place around the days of the winter solstice, December 21. They all seem to have some things in common: one is a soul-deep and most mysterious relationship to seasonal changes. Another is an urgent impulse to aid in bringing back the light. This is obscured by conflicting images, stories and rituals, but it is there, nonetheless. It is not surprising, then, that when I came to live in western Massachusetts, I felt the need for a winter festival to which all my friends would come, regardless of their personal faiths. This matter of differing faiths is no small problem nowadays, which you will find a challenge as soon as your three-year-old begins to play with others of the same age and eloquence. I had been deeply impressed by the beauty of a Winter Garden festi-

69

val done in Waldorf kindergartens, but I had no wish to violate the Waldorf spirit, nor "take down" the wonder a Waldorf teacher can achieve in the kindergarten classroom. Still, there was the need for a shared winter festival full of fun, friendship, reverence and mystery to help us all through the peculiar difficulties of this time of year.

So I set to.

First, I passed the word around the neighborhood that there was going to be something happening in my fenceless garden on December 21 that children might like to take part in. The time would be late afternoon twilight. There were no invitations, just word of mouth through the children.

I chose to work with a snow spiral, having seen and heard of spirals in the most amazing places all over the world. There is the most famous of all, of course, the Cretan maze of the Minotaur. There are the remains of some cut into the moss fields in Norway called Troy Towns. There are mosaic ones on hidden floors in cathedrals in Italy called "Journey to Jerusalem", which were used as penance instead of an actual journey to the Holy Land.

I chose to use snow in which to make my spiral in Massachussetts, even though I had no guarantee that it would fall by December 21 in that area. Each year I waited with a good deal of anxiety. Sometimes the first snow of the season did not fall until that very day. However, in the eight years I celebrated the festival, the garden was covered with at least six inches at the latest by mid-morning.

It's important to risk yourself for good things. But don't think I didn't panic sometimes!

Once the snow was deep enough, I went out to find a couple of children to help me trudge out a large slippery spiral in our open garden overlooking the icy Connecticutt River and the ancient mountains beyond. We stamped out a snowy spiral which must have been thirty feet across. The way wound inwards between two low snow walls to a center big enough for two persons to squeeze onto, and then went right on spiraling outwards. The inward and outward ways went side by side, but each created a totally different mood. Winter greenery and sometimes silver ribbons marked the edges between. A three foot tall candle was placed in the center.

The last thing was to find enough candles. I found that "emergency candles" served best. I never did know how many people would show up.

About four o'clock, when it began to turn to winter twighlight, families began to gather. Some I knew, some I didn't. We stood around the spiral forming a broken circle, awkward and cold. When there were enough of us, we galloped around the block in a straggling group shouting heartwarming songs at the top of our voices. After all, it was twilight on a very chilly day when mittens, earmuffs, heavy boots, parkas, scarves, even woolly face masks from the high mountains of Peru were not enough to keep out the cold.

By the time we got back to the spiral, everyone was singing or humming loudly. All sorts of songs from all over the world and from many religions and traditions found a voice. There were none, however, that couldn't be sung by everyone — the children themselves saw to that! The songs were about this cold dark time with its obvious need for light, both inner and outer.

When lots of people had ambled over, and it was dark enough, but not so much that the littlest ones might be frightened, then a teenager was chosen to go in and light the large central candle, someone who knew how to do it with some sense of drama, fun and responsibility: shivering to remind everyone of how cold it was, while crouching lower and lower, contracted by darkness, cold and fear.

At the center the teen lit the candle and stood up joyfully. It was the signal for the other children to spiral in. Some still needed to hold their parent's hand, but it soon was apparent that the adults all wanted to enter the spiral, with children or without. Everyone held a candle, still unlit, as they headed for the light at the otherwise darkening center. As each person arrived, they stopped to light their candle from the large one. The big people helped the little ones. Even the littlest child held a lighted candle. As people began to circle out, their mood changed.

By now, except for the crackling of the frozen trees, and the whistle of the wind, there was virtually silence in the open field. No longer any need to say anything: no healing songs, no instigating imaginations, just plain and simple wonder. The candleflame kept everyone erect. The magic of candlelight shone on radiant faces. The secret stirrings of the human heart turned dark eyes to shining stars. There was light radiating from each spiraling individual. At points on the snowy path, each person put their candles upright onto the snow, in little aluminum shields we had made so the wind would not blow them out. As each one did this, lighting the path for those who followed after, the spiral shone more clearly. At last everyone had slipped in trepidaciously and spiraled safely out. For a moment we stood in a full circle gazing at the results of our play – a spiral of light in the heart of vast darkness, one we had each helped make ourselves. Then, a last favorite song before we all went indoors to find hot apple juice and other treats to warm us up.

The last time I did this Snow Spiral, at least a hundred people found their way to it. As the years passed, they had come to expect the festival. They took part in it however they could, finding their own ways to do so. The treats became ever more lavish, the choice of song more inventive, the characterization of the winter mood ever more clear.

I never did send out invitations, never suggested potluck, never asked for songs or silence. It all happened, because on this darkest night of the year, the need to share was strong.

*The End*

# Ring Around the Roses

Ring a round the ro - ses,

Po - cket full of po - sies

A - shes! A - shes!

We all fall down.

The cows are in the meadow
Lying fast asleep
A-shes! A-shes!
We all get up again.

# Sally Go Round The Sun

Sal - ly go round the sun,

Sal - ly go round the moon,

Sal - ly go round the chim - ney pots,

On a Sat - ur - day af - ter - noon.

75

# Looby Loo

Here we go Loo - by Loo,

Here we go Loo - by Light,

Here we go Loo - by Loo,

All on Sat - ur - day night.

Put your right hand in

Put your right hand out, Shake a

lit - tle, a lit - tle, And turn your-self a-bout.

Verse 2. Put your left hand in, etc.
Verse 3. Put your right foot in, etc.
Verse 4. Put your left foot in, etc.
Verse 5. Put your nose in, etc. *

You can make up your own sequences and play as long as you feel the children are having fun.

# Here We Go
# Round The Mulberry Bush

Here we go round the mul - ber - ry bush, the

mul - ber - ry bush, the mul - ber - ry bush,

Here we go round the mul - ber - ry bush, On a

cold and fros - ty morn - ing.

2nd Verse: This is the way we wash our clothes, etc.
So early Monday morning.

3rd Verse: This is the way we iron our clothes, etc.
So early Tuesday morning.

4th Verse: This is the way we scrub our floor, etc.
So early Wednesday morning.

5th Verse: This is the way we mend our clothes, etc.
So early Thursday morning.

6th Verse: This is the way we sweep the house, etc.
So early Friday morning.

7th Verse: Thus we play when work is done, etc.
So early Saturday morning.

# A Tisket, A Tasket

# The Farmer's In The Dell

The   Farm   er's   in   the   dell,   The

farm   er's   in   the   dell,

Hi   Ho   the   der - ry   O,   The

farm   er's   in   the   dell.

2. The Farmer takes a wife, etc.
3. The wife takes a child,...
4. The child takes a cow,...
5. The cow takes a dog,...
6. The dog takes a cat,...
7. The cat takes a rat,...
8. The rat takes a cheese,...

# Oranges and Lemons

can - dle to light you to

bed, And here comes a chop-per

to__ chop off your head.

# London Bridge Is Falling Down

Lon - don bridge is fall - ing down,

Fall - ing down, fall - ing down,

Lon - don bridge is fall - ing down,

My fair la - dy.

1. Build it up with iron bars,
   Iron bars, iron bars,
   Build it up with iron bars,
   My fair lady.

   (repeat chorus)

2. Iron bars will bend and break,
   Bend and break, bend and break,
   Iron bars will bend and break,
   My fair lady.

   (repeat chorus)

3. Build it up with silver and gold,
   Silver and gold, silver and gold,
   Build it up with silver and gold,
   My fair lady.

   (repeat chorus)

790   Eliot, Jane Winslow
ELI   Let's talk, let's play

| | DATE DUE | | |
|---|---|---|---|
| FL | | | |
| | | | |
| | | | |
| | | | |
| | | | |
| | | | |
| | | | |
| | | | |
| | | | |
| | | | |
| | | | |
| | | | |

**The Bay School**
Box 269
Blue Hill, Maine 04614